The
Tide Book

Cover art: *I See You,* fiber art
Joanna Carlson Perea, Ebb and Flow Fiber Studio
www.ebbandflowfiberstudio.com

ISBN: 978-1-962405-34-8
Ebook: 978-1-962405-35-5

Library of Congress Control Number: 2025942942

Sheila-Na-Gig Editions
Russell, KY
Hayley Mitchell Haugen, Editor
www.sheilanagigblog.com

The
Tide Book

Poems

Vivian Faith Prescott

Sheila-Na-Gig Editions

Acknowledgments

Alaska Women Speak: "Fishcamp Kismet," "The Agreement,"
　　"The Driving Force," "Traces"

A Literary and Artistic Filed Guide to Alaska: "Dear Sitka
　　Periwinkle"

Cutthroat: A Journal of the Arts: "Island Water Quality Report"
　　received 2nd place, *Joy Harjo Award.*

DeLuge Journal: "Am I Awake Yet?"

Ilanot Review: "Occurring Frequently in the Wild"

Shantih Journal: "Fathoms"

Terrain Magazine: "Retroflection"

The Dodge Magazine: "Seawall" received the Best of Net
　　Award for poetry.

Tidal Echoes: "How to Report a Stranding," "Kymatology,"
　　"Map of Dogs," "My Father Departs With the Migrating
　　Birds Heading North," "Overlooking," "Reference
　　Station," "The Cabin Aubade," "The Role of Buoyancy
　　Forces"

West Trade Review: "How to Pulse With the World Like It's
　　Your Last Day"

Yellow Medicine Review: Women's Wisdom, Women's Strength:
　　"Grandmothers Are Cliché"

Some poems appeared in the chapbook *Marigram* From
　　Glass Lyre Press (2023).

Thank you to my poet partner Howie Martindale and my
writers' groups, the Blue Canoe Writers and the Drumlin
Poets, for taking the poet's journey with me on this big ocean
planet.

The Tide Book is dedicated to my family, including my father, who is now out fishing on the great cosmic ocean.

Contents

FRONTAGER
A person owning and often living in property immediately landward of the beach.

MARIGRAM
A graphic record of the rise and fall of the tide.

LAG TIDE
Periodic delay in the occurrence of high water and low water due to changes in positions of moon and sun.

BATHYMETRY

The measurement of water depths in oceans, seas, and lakes.

SEMIDIURNAL

The predominant type of tide throughout the world is semidiurnal,
with two high waters and two low waters each tidal day.

BENEAPED

Said of a vessel left aground following a spring high tide.

BODY TIDE

*Also called "Earth Tide": The displacement of the solid
Earth's surface caused by the gravity of moon and sun.*

NAVIFACE

The interface between atmosphere and ocean: sea surface.

FRONTAGER

*A person owning and often living in property
immediately landward of the beach.*

Siedde

"A strong Sámi identity enhances the mental well-being of Sámi."
—Klemetti Näkkäläjärvi

Rocky shoreline, bend of bay, seawall
built of boulders and stone stairs

leading up to my cabin. It was fair weather
and calm seas all year

so we picked berries through summer,
always a bucket of blueberries, stained lips,

bellies full of fish and now there's a deer
packed in the freezer.

The spirit of the ancients visited us here too—
there's a kingfisher sitting on the porch railing,

a hawk circles the beach, owls have been
hooting up these fall nights in nearby woods,

and the ravens and crows gather up
our mornings. Living near the seidde,

is a gathering place for resting spirits in transition—
       remove your hat,
       respect the quiet,
       know the sacred songs.

Let me repay the spirits for our gifts—
offer our bounty to others, leave an offering
of a bird-shaped stone.

Fishcamp Kismet

The small dead spider in my bedsheets
        is shaken out over my porch railing

at the edge of the sea.

Atop my seawall, a wild
strawberry plant from the Stikine River

blooms
little white flowers out of the skull

of a baby humpback whale.

On the beach below my fishcamp,
the wing bones of an eagle stretch out,

flesh-bare, as if ready to catch an updraft.

In the bluedark, a mouse falls from the sky
and thuds against my window.

These startles,
are a bit like a mink darting

into the crevasse in the seawall,
and sometimes they linger as long

as a hummingbird drinks nectar from
a bleeding heart.

Before these moments disappear,
        I often think: I will remember

how this wisp of eagle down swayfalls
like snow

onto my open palm. And then I don't.

There is a thick curtain
like old-man's-beard-moss

hanging from hemlocks, separating
my world from that other

shadowy dirt road,

that sweeps aside   again and   again,
without my having to draw back the strands.

Often it brushes away when
the weight of my footfalls crush

a raven's hat—the limpet—
and burst open popweed bladders.

Call me lucky, if you will—the old seawall

is the only thing protecting me now
            from the rush of tide,

and the strawberries
are ripening in the eye sockets of a whale.

Map of Dogs

"Where you find a dog's bones, man might not be far behind."
—Anthropologist

Our island's shapeline resembles a snow goose flying to the river flats
and I live in the crook of the goose's neck with two border collies,

Oscar and Kéet. I am the benchmark here, the permanent material
object, a marked point unto myself, and yet,

I traverse landmarks of neighbors by bend of road, line of crabapple
and meander of seawall. Forestry map, geological map, line map,

flood map, dog map—Patsy, Kiera, Baily, Finn, Scout and Daisy,
canine coordinates I walk to every morning. Dogs I've followed,

tossed a stick for, called up, even shooed away. If I could, I'd walk
beyond this map's margins, though, head east toward the mainland

to Bear Toe Cave, a hollow holding bear's metacarpal, raven's radius.
I'd find a spear point, bone awl, shell beads, and a tiny femur—

the oldest dog remains found in North America. Both dog
and human with a shared diet of seal, whale, and salmon.

When the band of ice melted, who led or followed whom to the cave?
And as the night-fire danced on stone, loyal companion,

a palm pressed atop your head, you curled together for warmth.
And perhaps it was that night or another when you followed

the well-traveled map of time to this moment, ten thousand years later,
and here I am charting our intersection: Dog and human

sitting on my porch next to the sea, and me scratching the dog's chin—
Good dog. Good. Dog.

Night symphony

is full of loon song
and heron squawk.

There's a snap in the alder,
a thud on my porch.

I welcome the night creatures—
open my cabin window
and a puff of something's breath rises
from the sea
and stirs up my goodnight.

The Agreement

Crows' static caws bid their goodnight
        like radio chatter and I am
tuning in to the day's end.

The local flock is heading to their roost
        but stop for stale breadcrumbs
dotting my porch railing next to the sea.

I am set back from the edge on a rickety
        camo lawn chair in front of my cabin
sitting so still as not to scare away the birds.

The evening light fades to crimson
        as a large raven joins in
on the beach below gathering tumbled bread.

This is my ordinary life here
        uncaged by office or children,
living within the spiral of tide and wind and sea.

Time here wavers and flows like a wrackline,
        leaving seaweed piles and threads
of fishing line and bits of broken shells.

My small cabin is part of this contract
        of intentional simplicity I've settled for
and this is its fine print—a single black feather

from an old crow is shed at my feet,
        flutters in wind, lifts as if it knows its path,
blows across the porch and drifts toward me.

Encounters

Glacier brushes winter into shadows and light.
My footsteps clack over stones
on the riverbank like an old wagon
traveling on ancient roads.

Everything is softening.
The ice sweats, history peels back.
The deer's jawbone rests atop a log
like a half-forgotten treasure.

This stench of disappearing is all around us,
and back home, news of mass graves, no funeral
processions, weeping,

this rusting of our glorious age. Yet out here
there's a chance encounter with a sleek otter
heading into the willow. This loud silence
is a vaccine if I listen close enough.

Island Water Quality Report

Our water faucets drip yellow, splash brown
and plop out occasional trout and allowable
contamination. Our teeth and hair shine
with disinfectant and so do our liver, kidneys,
and nervous system. We cook it up and sip it up
and spin it with our hoodies and underwear.

Island communion, we drink from it.

We get high south of town, Wrangell Mountain,
two reservoirs—high vulnerability rating, heavy metal high,
high for nitrates and bacteria and virus.
Take a sanitary survey. Stay informed. Form a band
on this rock and call it Water Supply. We swallow it and sing it—
take short showers, no fertilizers, or pesticides,
pick up dog poop. Adopt a watershed, make a flashy flyer,
flush tap water for 30 seconds before using.

Island communion, we drink from it.

Waterscent—treat the drink that stinks of haloacetic acids
and total trihalomethanes—infect with disinfect,
state official mentions older folks risk cancer. Gives example
of bladder cancer. Now, my dad lies still under the contraption
radiating his bladder and does weekly chemo. They tell him,
for the procedure to work, he must drink more water.

Island communion, we drink from it.

So This Is a Porch

Our deck is seaworn from salt and rain, sticky with alder resin, from the fledgling tree that grew up between rocks, now thriving beside the railing. So, this is a porch, as familiar as a tattered book, keeping the stories of a father and daughter, blankets wrapping their laps, sitting in lawn chairs with their binoculars, reading clouds and fish jumps.

This porch holds pages of old things, an 83 yr. old body, middle-aged dogs, a craggy and wood-split carving of an old fisherman leans against a porch post. This porch, where the hardback spine of moments are laid open, bookmarked by driftwood and memory, ready to record a tale—the mystery of a whaling ship fading in and out of fog, or the wonder of a bright meteor whizzing into the evening sea, or a submarine sighting.

Often, this porch binds a history printed in the ink of your father's memory, losing color, and still some stories return, again and again, predictable as figures in a tide book. Lately, you feel like this well-read book at the end of the day, living inside your dog-eared bones and coffee-ringed skin. And as spring's evening wilts, as you and your father head inside, you sense that you likewise have forgotten something, and there it is—beyond the window, in the fading light, an open notebook sits in the lawn chair, amid the blanket askew, the soft rain falling on letters.

Postcards From the Future Helix

Wish You Were Here: Invitations brought you,
grandparents, parents, children, an infant—
my grandmother—across the sea to a vertical shaft,
copper flecked dirt, a bedrock of lakeshore tears.

Having A Good Time: You worked mines for
a few years, but you were two chains, carrying
instructions: Don't breathe the dust of this life.
Don't put your feet deep into this earth.
Don't settle in.

The Weather's Been Nice: You fled again, joined
others on the Northwest coast, near harbors,
fishing boats, canneries. Felt like home
so you stayed….for a while.

We've Been Enjoying the Sights: Later, we met
at the backbone of us, encoded this new land—
spruce and hemlock forest, whales bubble-feeding,
herring so thick you could walk on the sea.

The Food is Great: We coil around one another still—
the way my fingers hold the rainbow smelt, cut
the knife through its belly and slices off its head.

We're Thinking of You: Now, I hear silver trinkets
jingling on our double helix sometimes, whenever
my body moves through this rainforest world just right.
I look behind me, in front of me, beside me, but your
footprints sink into the bog and then you're gone.

MARIGRAM

A graphic record of the rise and fall of the tide.

Retroflection

Press palm to sea, work the ocean,
        flatten it into a mirror

reflecting the Old Woman's light back to you.
        She is Ocean,

who wants what she wants—You've known this
        your whole life. She wants your body,

your cousins' body, your uncle's body,
        anyone's body. All these drownings

in your family history too numerous to speak of.
        She considers them gifts.

See her as she really is—Ocean simply wants
        her broken coral ribs mended, her sea hair

combed and braided, a care-taking as old
        as stories carved on cave walls,

and etched in stone on a nearby beach.
        After all, don't you recall her retroflection—

a current turning back on itself,
        how her hand reached up to yours,

in Brown Bear Bay, how you leaned over
        the boat's gunwales—there you are/were

with your fingertips swirling through
        flashing green diatoms, resisting

the urge to jump in, swim in her liquid light,
        while above you, a meteor

left a silver trail across August's black sky.

How to Report a Stranding

—For L, gone missing

Please let us know if you see her—
she was married to my nephew
and they have two kids.

If you see her, collect the data:
date, latitude, and longitude,
and take photos if you can,

though she never wanted to smile,
on account of her rotten teeth.
They say a stranded animal

is one who is dead on the beach
or in the sea or maybe even alive
on land unable to return to us.

I imagine you in the forest, peering
out from the alder at the searchers,
afraid to return to your human self.

Sometimes, though, I see you
washed away by incoming tide,
or entangled in a gillnet.

And I am there tossing a grapple,
my knife on the end of a pole,
ready to cut you free.

Overlooking

I want to live on like you,
rock-sheltered and etched as a porpoise

or killer whale with my adzework catching rain
and sunlight, lichen-patched,

beside a record of time—dots on a leaning rock wall
noting days and nights in an old winter village.

I want to animate shadows and waves like you
beneath overhanging rock, a canvas

for an image of a face or a paddling canoe.
I want to be ground stone and obsidian flakes,

red pigment binding with pitch, a vantage point
in these uncertain seasons. Oh, to be painted.

Bathymetry

I convince myself it's spring and walk
my waterbody into the sea. This Alaskan island

tradition is as old as my purple urchin-shaped
scarred knee where I fell off my bike

at 7 years old, turning a corner too fast
on a gravel road. Now, donned in barnacle

shielding shoes, shorts and t-shirt, my body
is a bathymetric map, a seafloor relief.

Above me, a bald eagle screeches like
an echo-sounder, the pulse of his cry reaches me.

As I wade past my knees the cold sea numbs
toes and my swishing hands—a scar

on my ring finger stings from a careless wash
across a broken window when I was a teen.

They say any seafloor is less measured than
the planet Mars, and here I am wading to my waist

pinging scars across my body-familiar
where I've mapped slopes and an oceanic trench

that's birthed my young, and a seamount, scarred
by stretch and movement like a seafloor plate.

The final dunk is the bravest part of this cold-dip
ritual, breasts and shoulders now submerged,

my scarred arm and my dented skull have
long been my companions. I turn on my back

and float face-up, knowing my skin is not
a protective membrane but a sieve,

and a sense that, indeed, this ocean knows
my every depth and slope and all my channel walls,

while the chill of brine rushes into me with
its shudder and thrill of an ancient blood memory.

Occurring Frequently in the Wild

The stories that shape you are restless,
in the coat pockets you've folded them into,

or rather stuffed them.

But there's a story loosening with a pull
of gloved hand from your pocket's warmth.

A story folded among grains of sand,

a whelk shell and lint, now lies beneath you
in a small puddle—on a trail next to the sea.

And there's a woman, a half hour behind you,

strolling in the light mist, leaves tumbling about,
and she has bent to pick up what she believes

is an origami boat and discovers it's really a note.

It's the beginning of story you were going to tell,
but could never bring yourself to write…

You jotted only a few words on paper.

And now the woman sits on a nearby bench,
not thinking about who happened to drop this

like a message in a bottle,

but the words, "my mother and the faded
and creased lines," written in ink—nothing more—

which is somehow, now, the note-rescuer's mother,

or perhaps someone else's mother in a photograph
of memory, dressed in pale yellow culottes

and bouffant hair sitting on a frayed blue blanket

on a beach near town, an infant on her lap,
as two toddlers dig in the sand nearby.

The mother's face is one that women recognize—

Eyes fathomed in a stare at something beyond
the eddy of time, beyond the sticky infant's hands,

and the green sea anemone in the rocky tide pool,

to the way water flows past the body wall,
and the infinite wave of feathery tentacles.

Kymatology: How to or Not to Ride the Waves

1. Ride like my Tlingit/Sámi/Filipino/Hawaiian grade-school
    grandsons in the Sitka surf. bobbing like seals. in their
    wet suits. on boogie boards. in November.

2. Ride like a seasickness mirage—commercial fishing
    offshore in the Gulf of Alaska. daughter sees brown bear
    spirits surfing the waves. offshore of Lituya Bay.
    in oral traditions—brown bear spirits live there.

3. Ride like 8-foot chop on the Stikine River flats—
    riding home with drunk river rats. hanging onto
    the runabout's dash. seats not bolted in. sliding
    to the stern. drunk men. me.

4. Ride the grief of another cousin, friend, fisherman,
    drowned. found tangled in a fishing boat's rigging.
    found floating. found beneath a toppled canoe.
    stuck under a dock. on an icefloe. along a beach.
    or not found at all.

5. Ride like my dream when I was a salmon. floating.
    floating, in a school of fish. reach to touch them.
    feel their fins and bodies swim by me. poet friend
    is standing on the beach, telling the Salmon Boy story,
    calling us home. home.

6. Ride like Uncle Howard through the story he told
    my kids—the time he and his son rode a mega-tsunami
    in his fishing boat over Cenotaph Island in Lituya Bay.
    highest wave ever recorded. hope like that. he said.
    ride your life like that.

7. Ride like the Man-of-Lit.uaa who shakes his blanket
    and sends waves knocking around Lituya Bay.
    my children's ancestral homeland. offer him/sea monster
    some tobacco. offer a lock of your hair when entering
    the bay.

8. Ride like a dance robe— Chaas' Koowu Tlaa—
   Mother-of-Humpy-Tail weaves a raven's tail robe—
   seismograph and mountains carved by a wave.
   waves woven with mountain goat hair. sea otter fur.
   put on the robe and dance the wave.

9. Daughter, ride the asphalt waves rolling over the
   Alaska highway—megathrust earthquake. you drove
   through. sonic boom. car shaking. drive faster. largest
   inland quake in 150 years. 7.9. rippling ocean.
   4 minutes in an apocalyptic movie, you say.

10. Ride like a freakish July storm. waves crashing into
    my seawall at fishcamp. wash sea spray from
    my windows. ride a year with storms. ride a year
    with no salmon. ride thoughts of the nearby glacier.
    melting.

11. Ride the uplift and subsurface rupture: My cousin Jerry,
    working the docks in Valdez, Alaska in 1964
    when a tsunami of mud and sea swept him away.
    9.2 earthquake. underwater landslide. water retreated
    from shore. swept back in. smashed a freighter.
    killed longshoremen. my cousin. and children.
    washed away the waterfront.

12. Ride November, ride spirits, ride chop, ride grief,
    ride dreams. ride toward home and ride away from home.
    ride taboos and dancing. ride asphalt and storms.
    ride the apocalypse. never still. ride the wind.
    ride the pull of the moon. ride our energy passing
    through this world. hang on. every one of us—
    ride our stories.

Kymatology: the science of waves and wave motion.

Oracle

You are a soothsayer in the new religion,
        a believer in the magic sphere
of your notebook. You are versed in the arts,

one who craves splashing
        blue ink and verses,
a diviner awakening the serene

into sharpened brainwaves. You push
        the ordinary into a new creation,
calling them come-hither and float them

across the page—rocks ringed in quartz,
        a branch of cedar roots
resembling an old woman.

You chant and divine the fullness of this
        coastal life with instruments of scribble—
blended with both cursive and print,

walking words beside enchanted song.
        Oh, sing that enchanted
song now, perform your own wonders—

and read that poem out loud.
        Poet, transform yourself
into a humpback whale

or the devil's club thicket draping the ravine.

A Marigram of Hope

Look, bright yellow stalks emerge from warm muck.
I bend to inhale their familiar scent.

Behold, an old man is ambling down the hospital hallway,
masked, gloved and gowned, while nurses and doctors
applaud his slow return to the world.

My feet press the dry roadside grass and I step over the ditch.
See the red branches on the blueberry bushes, note
a bud's first pink blush.

Look, we peer out the narrow window at our daughters and
grandchildren, holding signs: *We miss you. We love you.*
Rainbows and hearts and I try not to weep.

Today, and every morning for days now, with wing-sound
and honk, a pair of Canada geese fly by our porch.
We've named them after our airline flights: there goes
flight 64 and 65.

Look, the young woman and her sewing guild sew a thousand
cloth masks, and a grown daughter sits outside a care home
in a flowerbed talking to her mother through window glass.

See the man is in his shop fabricating a face shield. See
the family dancing and drumming on a dock next to the ocean.
See the stranger dropping a box of groceries off on a porch.

A nurse aid brings water to a bedside. See the mailman
opening the street-side mailbox, placing a letter.

There's a purple bud on the devil's club and fat robins
flit around the neighbor's grass near the outdoor rabbit pen,
and around the corner comes a parade

of elementary school teachers, each in their own sign-draped
cars, beeping horns, waving, cheered by students and parents
on the side of the road.

After days of herring snow and a few more days of sunshine,
the popweed plumps up on the beach. Everything is ripening,
and my elderly father sighs—*We're used to living
with the tide coming in and going out. We're patient people.
We can do this.*

Dear Purple Intertidal Sponge,

Yeah, I know you're thin and tightly packed. You're like a dozen small volcanoes ready to erupt, but hey, time to chill. The tidepool is not your only world. This beach is larger than you think it is. Everyone notices you, you say, but they don't know what you are, who you are. I know how that feels. You want to be seen. This is why I write, why poems shape themselves from pink to purple to lavender. You're known to reassort yourself if you've been damaged, so friend, maybe this is something you should consider now. Your original morphology was always beautiful, anyway. The sunstar and the blackeyed hermit told me so.

LAG TIDE

Periodic delay in the occurrence of high water and low water due to changes in positions of moon and sun.

Listening Station

Not slam of truck doors, moose stomps,
or red chrysanthemum fireworks, or snow

thudding off our roof, but energy waves
across the sea—Hunga Tonga-Hunga Ha'apai,

erupting in plumes of smoke, ash, a storm
of lightning, a tsunami.

Somewhere, it rains pebbles and darkness,
while I am in a river of warm sleep,

cradled between my typical audible range
of a wave rushing the seawall below

and a pygmy owl on winterbare branch.
Was it an onshore wind shaking my cabin walls?

Or a sonic boom from a mushroom cloud above
the blue Pacific?—I could not have dreamed that up,

while nestled into the belief of an ocean shared
in the damp night wrapped with breath.

Hydrographic

How is it that I found this universe in proximity
to a shoreline with edge waves nudging me to sleep at night.

> *Night sleeps in waves, nudging me nearer*
> *to the universe's shoreline.*

How is it that my blood's salinity is this poetic.
The pull of the moon pulls words from me each morning.

> *The morning pulls the poetic moon from me,*
> *pooling my blood's salinity into words.*

I call her Ocean, nothing extravagant, but say her name
out loud, bid her goodnight each night.

> *Night bids goodnight out loud, saying her name:*
> *"Ocean, Ocean."*

Each day I walk the zone between mean high and low water,
searching for the right rhythm and line.

> *The line moves with a rhythm of high*
> *and low water, searching for meaning.*

I pick up remnants of storm washed shells, broken bits of glass.

> *Glass, washed with storm, is a remnant of time.*

The fairy sparks glow in the boat's wake in front of my house—
I imagine diatoms need to dance.

> *Dancing needs to imagine diatoms in the boat's wake,*
> *a house awake and aglow, imagining fairies.*

The flood and glut of rain, an aftermath of squall and snowmelt—

ribbons of the Stikine River in sea-green and brown mud
along the shoreline.

> *The winter shoreline longs for ribbons of river mud*
> *and sea—each spring, flooding with squall and snowmelt.*

The morning's perspectives are tideland dynamic—eagles
bathe, crows and gulls drop clamshells to break them
open for breakfast, a thrush searches the seagrass for bugs.

> *I break open. in waves. in words. in high and low water.*
> *in u limpet's shell. in a boat's wake. in a spring flood.*
> *a tideland. I break open.*

Like Dreams to a Sleeper

"For the Sámi, the fire is more than light and warmth: it is a friend…"
—Emilie DeMant Hatt

Washed to the shoreline, your story seeks
a womb, a sheltering, even a spring fire

as a window to remember fragments
of offerings carried home within us.

But you realize a charm needs a spine,
a drum, a beating heart and shoulders,

a hand to set wood on flames, open
the eyes in the firewood. This telling

readies spirits to sing and story with us
all night, maybe learn a trick or two,

how to cut off bear's long tail, how to see
the old witch woman, stuck in pitch,

her beetle form flailing on the bright
night's moon.

The Driving Force

Falling older is not like growing, but a wave
of memories rolling up to press against my seawall.

Ageing is tumbling me over stones over this strip
of sand, blue mussels, and popweed.

There is no refuge from this rain and grayness,
this slack of tide.

What would I trade these years for?

My popular days of driving the meandering
roads of our island?

Me and two fellow mothers and our toddlers
fleeing the stink of drunken husbands.

Our tart and cranky secrets told amongst
ourselves, while wandering through neighborhoods

in a conversion van. We burned the fuel of days
and sometimes the evenings whenever they turned cruel

from a busted door hinge and an ax-thwacked
car hood. Maybe we felt time pulsing even then.

We surely knew the old stories of freak storms
and tsunami surges that washed over our dirt roads.

Maybe, though we accepted the power of oceans,
and swept along with it all, our fates, spinning us around
in the gyre.

Storm at Fishcamp

Praise to the dark windowpane, slant light,
a mournful echo of midnight.

Praise to songs of ancient pines, stitch-thin grass
swaying in porch light.

Praise to those who sleep sound, but especially
those who wander outside like me,

socks wet from decking, sweater clutched tight,
our ancestors' memory sharp beneath skin.

Praise to sea witches, serpents, the lurking,
the sleek, wet, knobby, the big round-eyed,

water breathers, and air suckers. Praise to the known,
and unknown, the near and beyond,

the breath I draw in and hold tight, the sigh
exhaled, drowned by wind.

Praise to conjuring storm, somewhere knots untied.
Praise to splash and jangle, clank,

and bend and wobble enfolding me. Praise
to heron's squawk bruising a path down my spine.

Praise to this storm, seawall beneath my feet,
five fingers clutching porch rail,
a white plastic chair bobbing in the waves.

Fists

—On the morning after the 2016 election

I squeezed the dark, gray clouds
with my fist this morning—

Rain saturated the island.
I walked out into the sea, knee deep,

and picked up a fistful
of rocks and flung them out into the ocean.

They dropped heavy, spinning in a circular motion
their ripples fanned out,

as one circle grew and another and another,

the behavior of water dependent on pressure
weight and motion— I did this. We did. You.

And as the ripples tongued the beach
their sound keened, accompanying the rain

shrouding islands like a mourner's veil,
covering the mirrored sea

and the small lake at the end of the road.

This rite I performed, punched the air upward,
held anger until it formed ash, pressed it further

into glass and scattered it about.

Surfacing

Breath awaits with a lungful of sunlight atop a green sea.
You, two-legged, observed me and named me #539.
But I am *Old One of the Ocean*, birthed five calves, tail first
and buoyant, with midwives nudging them to first breath
where rain washed their skin. Later, we rubbed sharp
barnacles from tiny bodies and led our young to swirls
of herring and pink krill, taught them to tail-slap and leap
from the surface.

My five calves gifted me descendants. Grandchildren,
you call them—Little Ancients, I say. I witnessed their pale
gray skins, soft from bellies, each lifted to the surface—
first breath, first lick of daylight.

A life of remembered songs, I followed others on tracks
of sea. My scarred tail, scraped and bitten, evidence I survived
predators, storm, ice, and acidic ocean. That day, clouds pulled
a shroud across hemlocks and kittiwakes skimmed island cliffs.
Instinct: salt-scented air moves through passageway to trachea,
passes through an air passage and fills lungs. Dive. Swim
among Little Ancients tumbling through gray-light.

Warming sea, algal blooms, chemistry and sound changed.
Ambient noise. Spray and bubbles, dolphin clicks. Rising.
One breath. All reflex. Cruise ship. Tourists with binoculars
spotting for spouts. Ship's bow bearing down. Last breath.
no breath. Floating. Hush.

Alaskan whale, a grandmother of three, killed by a ship strike.

Now, I am vapor in a waterspout: Lying on the beach among
popweed and gumboots, the brown bear is pulling flesh,
bald eagles circle. Low water and flood stream are swelling
and breaking, joining me to this harmonic constant,
where the ocean cannot taste its own tears and the membrane

of sea is thin. Listen. An echo off the ocean floor. Soundwaves
travel through the sound channel. Come to the surface again—
in an ice-filled bay—Little Ancients are lobtailing and
spy-hopping. A blue berg rolls on the silty sea. I am buoyant.
Someone holds me up. I re-surface and inhale my first breath.

You Are Here

Humans pressed red ochre handprints to cave walls,
carved spirals and a raven stealing the sun in glyphs
on the beach near town.

My 83-year-old father uses a black Sharpie and writes
his initials on his Penn 49 salmon reel, on his ax handle,
a hand sander, a chainsaw,

and on his red lunch cooler. He etched and painted
a salmon on the end of a canoe paddle and hung it
on the wall and he still carves

cedar pegs, a lost art, because no one uses them
to fish for commercial salmon anymore. He says
salmon love the cedar-scent

and will bite on a herring bent with a peg. Father,
you are here now, although the art of leaving
your body has slowed.

The doctor said it could be months before the cancer
takes you out in the skiff to the "fishing hole in the sky"
as we've been naming death,

and if we're lucky, as fishermen often are, maybe
you'll have a year. In your lifetime, you've left
your imprint on almost everything.

Across our island, you built signs, cabins, and trails,
picnic tables and outhouses, for the U.S. Forest Service.
But there's not an artistic bone

in your body, you say, while sanding a burl to hang
on an outdoor wall, and some days, my ears dangle
and sway with green,

beady-eyed, hoochie squids that you fashioned into earrings for me from your salmon trolling gear.

Dear Goldeneye

Where you nest is none of my business—you've always been independent. Born swimming, walking, foraging, and feeding for yourself. I admire that. Not like the songbirds or raptors. You don't seem to need a man, preferring the presence of other women. That's the kind of friend I favor, making use of a deadfall in the boreal forest, any tree cavity will do. You make everything a home. Tend to your babies. I love it how you're not afraid to dive underwater, yet you're quiet like me and I've enjoyed our visits, how we can just sit with our friendship, telling stories and when it's time for you to leave, I cry at the sound of your whistling wings.

BATHYMETRY

The measurement of water depths in oceans, seas, and lakes.

The Inside Passage

"Look down on the sky ocean."
—Aillohas, Sami poet: Nils-Aslak Valkeapaa

This solitude is liquid, a weary stream
tracing distant journeys.

Even the empty fish-cleaning table
is slipping into an echo.

What if time spooled with
the tempo of a melt season

back to our own screaming origins,
how we met this life with eyelids open

about to slide into this psycho ocean,
this warm climate, this inhaled disease.

What is there to offer up to
the gods now?—

soft apples and tasteless honeydews
barged up from Seattle,

a spruce root basket woven in this strange year?
Maybe a desk stacked with unfished poems,

because all I can focus on lately is adjusting
to new conditions and avoiding predators.

Fathoms

—For Alex and other activist teens living in small Alaskan towns.

This is a girl among icebergs, on a school trip in the bay of Big Thunder, when the glacier caught rifle shots from Florida, from Connecticut, from Virginia, and the ice fractured and calved, came crashing down like a breaching whale. This is a girl who is never far from where rifles are kept in corners, on bookcases, in closets. Last weekend she went moose hunting and today, with her iPhone, she filmed a kid in her class, yelling: *I'll shoot up the school*. He'll do it. He will. The teachers tell her: *Be quiet, don't show that clip to anyone. He has the right to privacy*—the school didn't expel him. This is a girl accustomed to the sound of rifle shots. She harvested deer before she even turned sixteen. She's pounded deer skin drums, eaten deer jerky, smoked, and jarred meat, shot a large halibut, even. This is a girl who rests her head on her desk at school and tries to understand, to fathom, to witness. She wonders about being alone while not being alone. She listens for the echolocation, passes a note to another student––*Walk out. Speak out*. Do something, this girl. She circles the note through the class like a bubble net. She knows whales feed in groups, this girl does. And when she decides to sound, her fluked tail rises, trailing seawater, and she takes the hand of another girl beside her, and that girl takes another's hand and another and another. This is a girl who doesn't know how long they should stay beneath the surface, but this is a girl who can fathom depth, a measure of length beneath her family's fishing boat. A fathom is six feet down into her cousin's fresh grave—his wounds upwelled to drown him. This is a girl who can hold all their breaths for as long as it takes. There's an ancient sea within her and she's seen her grandfather measure his halibut skate, a line running the length of a gravel driveway. This is a girl who rides fathoms in spiral paths, the evening light on the sea—a girl who knows the humpback whale dives a hundred feet down into the dark calm—a girl who still believes a single fathom is the span of her outstretched arms

The Cabin Aubade

Somewhere my dreams are tangled in sheets
and she is still lying beside me.
Somewhere, night is carved with river and sand,

and on the other side of the veil, a cabin is edged
in gold moonlight. In that world, there is another
tender body, another love,

though the same small patch of fireweed still grows
next to the porch and the cottonwood leaves
still turn in the wind.

All night, star girls danced in their own circle,
above us, to flickers of song notes, but now
threads of dawn weave through forest.

Perhaps it was only an ancient longing, stirring hope
as medicine for despair with a dreamfire's snap
and warming of hands.

But not before the longing caressed love's sheen
along her shoulder, then slipped though the cabin door
without creaking, and ducked out from under

shadows, and walked a pine laden path toward
a breaking sky, toward this day, pink with blushing.

A Waste of Time Is Cliché

On my deck next to the sea, *Time* flitters from morning
to afternoon as my father and I listen to robins and crows
and let fishing story after story uncoil fathoms.

Time is tossed here at my fishcamp on a Mariners game—
my father in his bathrobe, grimacing occasionally from
cancer pain, making comments about the pitcher's arm,
while dueling hummingbirds' wings whir at the feeder
just beyond an open glass door.

Time gobbles oven Swiss steak these days, and rib-eye steaks
on the grill, the halibut pizza, and today, the shepherd's pie.
My father's favorite meals, hours in the making,
as if every meal will be carried to the funeral pyre.

I could be vacuuming beach sand from my cabin floor,
stuffing a sleeping bag into the washing machine,
but minutes are dulled and tucked in a tackle box,
a threadbare rope of seconds, and days like a limp frond
of seaweed, wilt in too much rain.

Fallowed *time* nowadays slices through a small block
of cedarwood. My father, a knife between his fat fingers,
moves the blade downward, making thin cedar pegs
for baiting up trolling gear, meant for bending
the herring just so—My father will never use them.

Time huddles in close, slips the knot of story—my father
and his sister are young children on their father's troller,
learning to use knives, carve cedar pegs, while his own
father hauls in salmon after salmon, the trolling poles out,
lines down, the herring peg bending the bait, the silver
herring twirling, flashing beneath the sway of a green sea.

Unruffled Acoustics

One day, I went out into the heartbeat of the world
and listened for the faint sound of the fairyfly

and the echo of the blue whale.
Today, I figured living a good life was about listening—

the lull of waves, the yapping neighbor's dog,
the crows laughing in the spruce behind my cabin.

The day wandered along with sound, whirled itself up
in wind and rain, shuffled along the deck

with the scrape of bench and bucket roll.
The uproar of the world also went on around me,

the bulge and pulse of war and virus, gunshot, and startle.
Yet, there I was, a part of it all, tucked into the shoreline,

hunkering down, pulling the wool of evening over
my own pulse. And when I settled in

and shook beach sand from my sheets, petted the dog's
nose goodnight, there was not one shiver

of knock or image of rocking sea, but only a faint thought,
I was certain would not rustle up in the morning,

that all day, though I leaned and listened into the whoosh
and whistle and thud, sound sensitive creature I claim to be,
I heard nothing.

Tilting Away From the Sun

How beautiful are hanging lichens
drenched in glistening raindrops.

Everything is beautiful I tell
myself, on this morning, at this moment,

but the prone patient, in his tubes and wires,
his image swirls across the puddle I'm walking through.

And there's another image, caught in the straggling
berry bushes, a child's face on Twitter,

announced she'd died of covid-19 a week ago.
Where was I a week ago, but fretting

about what's coming—frozen locks on my car door,
the leak dripping from the bathroom ceiling,

the white buckets rolling across our driveway,
as a child was falling through this life.

So many families falling at Zoom-linked bedsides.
And still, I walk through another rippled puddle

making my way past a rhododendron bush,
an evergreen with a single red leaf,

and an orange devil's club leaf, still holding on
in this last predicted storm.

How beautiful our road
scattered with gold mottled alder leaves

swaying in the morning breeze
like butterflies at my dogs' feet.

The Age of Barnacles

—To us home caregivers navigating the pandemic.

Summer yawns across the sky, migrating morning
clouds aside and there's a shift in my calcareous shell.
Every day, I awaken and consider if it's a mistake

to reach the edge of my intertidal zone. Fear's tendon
still holds like a bull kelp stem to the seafloor.
There's a gap between wanting and the solace of the
wrackline.

I am adapting to this altered life like a barnacle body,
my cirri clinging onto anything nowaday—a kind word,
a sea sponge, a daily video chat with a grandchild.

But lately something has beckoned me out from grief
but it's still an early stage in my strange evolution.
For now, call me common, call me oceanic,

call me a grandmother—we're an ancient group.
We are the ones called to sift through the grit
of distance and ache, to recall our survival stories.

I think of the carpets of barnacles across the planet,
abundant and widespread are their remains,
all the dead, their epoch denied, likely forgotten

in the upwelling of this cold deep sea. Has someone
kept a list of names for all the small flags that were planted?
The moments of silence are like waves,

prayers are said and sent to the depths of our oceans
and the highest reaches of tides. Let us remember.
Let us feel the swell.

Dear Surging Glacier,

I can relate. First there is the quiescent season, where there was no noticeable change, and you went about your day, the gray hairs, the lines along your eyes and mouth, this body thickening all at a glacial pace. You didn't seem so highly sensitive then, but lately, I've noticed some drama—an ice-fall, some popping, and grinding. They say our constant *is* change—we are inherently dynamic. So, I just wanted to say, hold on, friend, there's going to be more melting than accumulation as the surge wave moves down, heading for that final outburst. I am here for you.

SEMIDIURNAL

The predominant type of tide throughout the world is semidiurnal, with two high waters and two low waters each tidal day.

Seawall

Nothing
separates us/me
from the sealion. I catch his breath-scent.

If I don't hear the ocean next to my pillow,
all is not well in the world.

The small stone that I swear was gold,
I stuffed into the seawall—
The ocean said it was hers.

Mink skitters along the rock wall,
startling the dog.

How many fish have looked up at me
looking down at them?

How many fish have seen me
tossing wish rocks from my porch into the sea?

The Role of Buoyancy Forces

On any given day, clouds gather as mountain goats
        and running dogs, and occasionally a giraffe
or swimming salmon.

Another day, stripes of mare tails whip the sky.
        Today, hematite-dark clouds barrage us
with rain and wind across the beach.

The weatherman insists our daydreams
        are really cirrus, stratus, and cumulus,
and we are doused with a nightmare

as news of another boating accident—five dead—
        fishermen trapped, found floating,
and not found at all.

How we endure a spirit-breaking summer
        while in our boots, sloshing through puddles,
yet unable to fish, the wind

wavering us like cloud-reflections on sea.
        El Nino means more storms—our receipt
for floating through the Anthropocene.

Our cabin heat remains on this summer
        and there's a fresh June snowfall
on mountain peaks, and somehow,

we still believe we have a hold
        on this edge of an overturned skiff.

Spare Hallowed Rations at the Store of the Living

Blessed are my cans of cream of chicken soup,
can after can stacked on the commercial grade shelf
in my cabin.

Blessed are the cans of milk, the boxed milk,
the bag of powdered eggs. Very blessed is
the stack of Spam, apocalypse surviving cans.

Especially blessed is the market shopper,
with my list in hand, selecting whole wheat
English muffins despite the big *NO*
whole wheat muffins written on the list.

Blessed you are, reader or not-reader of lists,
shopper of my sustenance, masked or not masked,
jabbed or not jabbed, holder of all my devout nutrition.

Blessed be my virtuous shelves, stacked with flour,
noodles, and rice, blessed be my big bags of dog food,
my case of store brand green beans.

Blessed be our mail checkers, and dropper offers,
and ghost kiss-blowers, air huggers and wavers.

We, the sheltered old fishermen by the sea,
the cracked open-hearted, the veteran, the vein
and artery clogged, insulin resistant and stitched up,
shall remain virus free for now and be blessed and blessed.

Coriolis Force

To you, inhabitants of my cells,
I am still a small rock

teetering on a faultline,
a root fingering out beneath

a thin layer of soil,
I was expected to expect death,

to rage into that unknowing space,
to unfasten my skin

from this weeping.
But here I am instead,

a moon-drowned body sitting
on my porch next to the sea,

in the cool night,

still casting faint shadows,
wiping glacier dust from

the soles of my feet.

Intertidal

—After Linda Hogan

Be like the barnacle that fastens
to the slick boulder, stick to your
intertidal habitat or be the one
who leaps over tide pools.

Be like a frilled dogwinkle
and use your teeth-covered tongue
to suck out barnacle guts, or be its shell
making music on a windchime.

Be like the plate limpet, fill children's
pockets. Resemble a beautiful nipple,
a sombrero, or an Unungan bentwood
hunter's cap. Be a Yéil Saaxu, a hat
for Raven the trickster.

Am I awake yet?

Am I awake yet? I floated through a year of dreams and
the silver kettle after my morning walk welcomes me
through the front door once again. I shake off the rain,
pondering a thought—there's been a whale skeleton
at the bottom of the sea all winter long and a black bear's
bones have fallen through a carpet of moss. A woodpecker's
wing-torn body and the remains of a vole are rotting
somewhere—Everything leaves a trace. So will this—
Our brother-in-law died from Covid-19 on Christmas Eve,
and I learned to yoik* from a woman on another continent.
Every few weeks, we shook our bodies awake, grounded
our feet, chanted the crow, the wind, and reindeer.
Notes wavered and growled across time zones and
opened our throats. This is *awake*, isn't it? Some nights
I swear, being wide-awake is terrifying—lately it seems
the wind merchants have sold all their knots and the body
count keeps going up and up. Nearby, a tree leans over
a nearby road ready to fall and winter is here yet again.
It's like something is rousing me from torpor and I can't
shake the dream—there's a recurring one—I'm a salmon
floating in a school of other fish on the Stikine River delta
and a poet I know is on the beach telling a story.
With each wave of his hands through the gray mist,
he summons us to the creek beside him. In the dream
I don't want to wake up and I am melancholy when I do.
But this is just like me—I'm always reading messages:
a stone shaped like a foot, a driftwood shaped like a seal,
and a heron flying overhead so close I see the underside
of her blue wings. I blink myself awake.

*Yoik is a traditional Sámi chant

Sea Stars

I once knew a girl who shrank away.
        I saw her last in the subtidal cafe,
wearing a sunflower dress, her head lolling

on her spindle body as she slow-walked
        across the floor—
her unnatural body twisting, lesions, jelly like

a giant pink star, mottled star, ochre star
        and sun star—star light, star bright,
why are you wasting away tonight?

*

One Thanksgiving at a friend's house,
        I cleaned her vomit off the toilet rim
before I used her bathroom. The friend,

days before, told me her anorexia
        was something she had
when she was young, and she wasn't worried—

said she could resort to starving
        if she ever needed.

Leather star, vermillion star, bat star, rainbow
        and sun star—syndrome spreads
from one species to the next.

I measure my wrists, forefinger to thumb,
        trace my shoreline every day.

Outbreaking

On record, beyond our view,
        is always another apocalypse—
a star is now fading into a galaxy's shadow,

        and the last of an unseen species
is trodden beneath our feet.
        Lately, I can sense

there's an ancient current at the edge
        of myself
and the wind is washing over me

        to clear my thoughts.
Somehow, I need to know if there is
        a pattern to all of this—

I can see a crack in the purest of ice
        and already the last twig
on the Great Earth Tree has snapped

        under the weight of our sorrows.
As this year turns, I'm ready to sing,
        dance, drum, or recite anything

to spook the horsemen, send them fleeing.
        Now hand me the knife
to cut the threads of this woven gloom

so I can let the bright days in again.

Dear Water Jellyfish,

Please forgive me for holding you. As a child I needed something, any life, to hold onto. I was gentle, I know. As gentle as a five-year-old can be. You, likely in your medusa stage, gelatinous disc washed ashore, bioluminescent at your best, I was amazed, holding you in the palm of my small hand, gazing into your body. Sweet Water Jellyfish, I can remember you taught me amazement and wonder and gentleness. I set you down on the sand, maybe I freed you in the ocean. I'm sure I did. I still see you once in a while, but I walk gently around you now. Sometimes, if I think you're struggling, I set you gently into the sea. I'm wondering if you still remember me.

BENEAPED

Said of a vessel left aground following a spring high tide.

Grandmothers Are Cliché

—said a writing mentor

Grandmothers crochet and take in four grandchildren and give their daughters breathalyzers before they can see their kids. Grandmothers write copy for Amazon. Grandmothers have PhDs and MFAs and take care of their PTSD soldier husbands who return from Iraq kicking and screaming at them, pulling the covers to hide in the dark. Grandmothers' houses are robbed by their meth-head grandsons. Grandmothers sift through the garbage dump on the beach for tossed away metals and broken glass to make art. Grandmothers weave dance robes. Grandmothers are CEOs signing million-dollar language revitalization checks. Grandmothers carve dance masks from alder. Grandmothers harvest fireweed and mountain goat hair and pull cedar bark from trees. Grandmothers blow deer calls made of leaves. Grandmothers play with Ouija boards. Grandmothers fish for salmon. Grandmothers hunt moose. Grandmothers teach 2nd grade. Grandmothers gut deer. Grandmothers lie on the muskeg on their bellies, picking cranberries. Grandmothers fall in love with the young men who work around their houses for the summer. Grandmothers chop wood. Grandmothers practice tsunami evacuations. Grandmothers fall in love with women who sculpt owls. Grandmothers. Grandmothers wipe blueberry-stained fingers and blood from their hands—periods flowing and ending, salmon hearts pulsing in their palms. Grandmothers clutch their empty bellies. Grandmothers fill them up. Grandmothers trace scars across their chests and comets across the sky. Grandmothers hold Grandfathers or Grandmothers in the bluedark night. The bluedark night holds Grandmothers. Grandmothers carry grandchildren to medivac planes. Grandmothers feed great-grandfathers, feed grandkids and great grandkids. Grandmothers join wet-t-shirt contests, wash the faces of their brain-dead sons and slice open halibut.

Grandmothers change flat tires on Honda Fits. Grandmothers love the scent of outboard exhaust. Grandmothers offer salmon casseroles at the thresholds of the newly deceased. Grandmothers remember names and then forget names. Grandmothers read Mad Magazine. Grandmothers stand in the dark with one another listening for the humpbacks' song. Grandmothers love their beer. Grandmothers collect porcelain Japanese dolls in glass boxes. Grandmothers march through town carrying signs to save rivers, stop dams and mining. Grandmothers wear hoodies. Grandmothers wear brown rubber boots. Grandmothers smoke cigarettes next to grandkids while eating Mystic Mint cookies and watching Fox News. Grandmothers pick the tails off thousands and thousands of shrimp. Grandmothers sigh when herons fly close to their heads. On the beach, Grandmothers trip on slick wet rocks and fold themselves into holy rites, slicing their cheeks on igneous—Grandmothers lie there waiting in the tidal interval for the duration of rise and the duration of fall.

Resurgence

—In response to the second wave.

Weather becomes winterdark,
        seabeaten and mooncold
surrounding our house at the edge
        of this troubled dark.

We are simply caretakers
        of our own fleeting tracks,
yet where our line of site clears,
        there/here we are—

full of our ocean-selves
        until we discover a sea-soaked
eagle feather limp on the beach—

It's a sign, we consider,
        as our stormworn bodies scuttle
 back to safety once again.

On Being the Stikine River

Let's ponder our neighbor's ways
       of braiding and twisting itself.

It reshapes us every year,
the way we move across sandflats
       the way the edges of us

shift and overturn.
This river, this way of knowing
       whirlpools and cottonwood scents

moose tracks in sand,
and log jams,
       it is the nature of its nature

to debride our wounds,
to sift beneath our soles,
       embed in our scalps.

We love its danger, this wild
thing we can't name
       but that the old language teemed

from its tongue—
bitter, silty water,
       a dog biting its tail.

When it's over,

our boat will be filled with fuel
and silver herring will be thawing
in a bucket on the stern.

When it's over, Grandson will be toddling
on the beach, his arms full of orange seaweed.

When it's over, my fingers will be stained
with blueberries and a daughter will be beside me,
filling her bucket, and we will drop berries
onto the soft mossy ground.

When it's over, several generations will be eating tacos
on our porch in the sunshine and a grandson
will float on an innertube in the sea below—
He will wave at us and pretend he's a killer whale.

When it's over, I'll hold a new grandchild
and his fingers will wrap around mine.

When it's over, grandchildren will build blanket tents
and eat candy, and playing cards and potato chips
will scatter across my floor,

spill out onto my deck and, there, a sly crow
will perch on the railing, same as he always did,
when it wasn't over. He will invite his crow friends
like he always does, and I will feed them stale potato chips,
like I always do.

Goldeneye Morning

Ducks float near barnacled shore,
and breeze ripples sea as each wrinkle
moves closer to the faint sun.

This day, though, warm enough
to sit outside sweatered with moments
of sky, white clouds brushing

snow-dusted mountains, is what I need
beneath my tender skin, to fill my
inner archipelago.

I wrap my hands around a warm cup
of coffee scent and salted sea, take notice
of Barrow or Common—things my
father taught me—look closer.

Note the triangle head, round white spot
or crescent-shaped behind the bill.
The ducks dip their heads into the sea

hunting for blue mussels and sea stars.
What is it you search for? I say aloud,
straightway, wondering if I am asking
the ducks or asking me.

Swells a Chant That Heals My Mind

The balm of evening is a solace from grief.
The sky darkens to granite.

I have found that in these days, even the mountain is weepy.
The sky darkens to granite.

What would it take to level us?—a tidal wave, a landslide, a death.
The sky darkens to granite.

No one has provided me with a handbook for aging
        that doesn't end with The End.
The sky darkens to granite.

Here, I am on the fringes of this hollow year and still
        I am turning the upside of leaves,
        and still laughing with crows.
And the sky darkens to granite.

And still I am flesh, still I am enlivened by
        inhaling the perfume-scent of rain.
And the sky darkens to granite.

*Title from a line from *Rain Fugue* by Jessie Redmon Fauset (1882-1961)

Send It to the Moon!

—For my father in hospice at home.

Who trimmed the wick of my father's mind,
as he awoke after a day of cancer stupor and doze?
My brother, flicking the TV remote to find a movie,

lit up the big screen with a listing of a documentary
about the moon. *Let's send the smokehouse to the moon!*
my father declared from the rocket that is his recliner.

For a moment, confusion whirlpooled its thick fog
in our cabin, until my brother said, *But Dad, send*
the smokehouse to the moon? There are no fish on the moon.

My father, always the problem solver, the expert builder
of custom smokehouses, the fisherman, who can carve
a one-eyed Little Joe or bend a Hoonah Spoon,

and slice a thin cedar peg to curve a herring to swim
in perfect salmon-catching symmetry, said to my brother,
For the moonfish, of course.

When the tide is coming in during a supermoon, I've seen
herring dance, glinting on the surface of sea, so don't
moonfish exist, *can't* they exist in the memory

of the dusty moon, and in the radiant orb that is now
my father's fish-loving brain? And so, while having
coffee this morning, my own mind invented a rocket

to carry a smokehouse to the moon. There, I set it up
on the edge of our physical bodies' cosmos and I summoned
all the flashing moonfish. And me and my father,

following a thread of earthlight, trolled our skiff across
the wide expanse of the Known Sea.

*First line inspired by a line from poet Vahan Tekeyan, "Prayer on
the Threshold of Tomorrow."

*Known Sea, Mare Cognitum, the "Sea that has Become Known."

Oceanic Ars Poetica

Sometimes, my poems are long waves
        travelling across the ocean,
        over the sea of bedcovers.

Before I try to sleep, I sense this gravitational
        muse exerting her force on me,
        and I pull the window-shade higher,

set my notebook on the nightstand,
        ready the pen for this
        earthbound ritual.

Every year the moon moves 1.5 inches away
        and perhaps I sense the movement,
        that those spaces are blank lines,

uninspired days, writer's block.
        So if and when sleep comes,
        there'll always be a blinked awakening,

when the highest point in the crest
        of wave reaches my shore,
        as my blue ink pen touches my notebook.

Scientists explain the ocean is shaped
        like a football with its narrow
        end pointing at the moon.

But I see a shaman's oval drum,
        pulling the poem from my sleep,
        out from the depth of my coral-like bones.

And by the time the tide turns
        to return to the far side,
        on the wave of a night tide,

a hunger for words has stretched
        every mussel alive, to breathe
        moonlight through my skin.

Dear Many-Eyed Ribbon Worm,

Yes, it takes many eyes to see, friend. And you have always seen through my deceptions. Seen right down to the bottom of my ocean. You've seen the plastic bottle I tossed in the garbage. Saw the cardboard I forgot to burn, the haphazard way I stepped on the moon snail nest, not seeing it there. Many-Eyed friend, what can we do about it now, though? What good is seeing if there are no solutions. And let me ask you: Is the world still beautiful in the morning when you open your many eyes? Do you get tired of seeing at the end of the day? Dear friend, remember to take care of yourself and may your sight always be filled with seawater.

BODY TIDE

Also called "Earth Tide": The displacement of the solid Earth's surface caused by the gravity of moon and sun.

Oceanic

Frost forms ancient patterns in puddles,
brown leaves curl from cold on the thin alder.

This cabin perches like a blinking moon
atop our seawall. Moonlight pools atop sea,

clings like glitter to porch rails and stone steps
as nightfall seeps through cabin walls.

Awakening at midnight with waves of tide
glimmering on the ceiling, the bay's moonlight

scatters across my bed and I pull covers down
and let sealight ripple on skin,

and like a small feather adrift,
I revel in shimmering waves of light,

until I sink into the pillow of sea, falling
into that deep trough, into the dream of dark brine.

Everything you need to know about Galactic Sámi migration from Sápmi to Michigan to Oregon to Alaska

No reindeer, no sleds, no boats or skis, but water pipes,
wiring, coins, cookware, lightning rods, and shipbuilding.
Atomic number 29 in the mine. There are fascinating
photos of the mine rush, and the dead are falling 3,000 feet
into a mine shaft. Stick with me, my family. Pursue genealogy
and your geology. Dragged or followed? What's the difference?—
We left graves behind. We were always lassoing something,
catching everything, even another boat. Catch a fever, catch
a current, a wife, a husband, a missionary's zeal, catch the north
wind under your hat. Ride it to Alaska, to the small cannery
on the shore, to the bunkhouse, the mess hall, the slime line.
Learn the gill net, the fish trap, the purse sein and how to troll.
Hand all the knowledge down in town, in bred, in bed,
in me—1.4 mg of copper per kilogram of my body weight,
from the troller, to fishing permits, the fish nets, the copper
bottom-paint, to the boat's rotting planks, to me standing here
on our garbage dump beach in Alaska, salvaging copper tubing
and wire from a derelict troller. There's a copper doorknob
in my hand and like a noaide I'm twisting it over and over as if
to open that door again and trigger a supernova from a massive
star in the Milky Way, shape-shifting us once more into ancestors
traveling around and around the earth, telling a ring of our stories—
Remember the daughter of the moon—wife of the northern lights,
she embroidered a blanket of stars.

Lunicurrent

Close the shade of wondering,
lock tight curiosity's salty air,
        brush away rain,
but leave the door ajar.

For love always wanders at night,
unable to sleep
to the melody of that unmissable breath—
the sound of whales.

Standing on my porch
in the dark, staring into
        the ink-black ocean,
instinct tells me to break this locked-in gaze,
just turn and go back inside my cabin,
back to the cave of warm covers.

But here, there is a wildness
        walking the beach,
and if I tilt my head just right,
I can hear her wet footsteps,
I can feel her hand still on my shoulder.

Transformed Beauty in the Algae Garden of Delight

I live with my slug family of dish-shaped, keyholes,
      hoof and slipper snails.

Some of us dance on feather boa kelp, are turbaned
      and sway on a pole of surf grass.

In this intertidal world, I mucus-trail place to place,
      attach to a rock, cling firm and steady,

wave-swept through the drift of days. Someone
      wrote a poem about my peculiarities,

about loving a limpet. I was born male then
      transformed to female. Don't be shocked

by nature's dazzling show. If necessary,
      I'll morph-pretty, back to a male again.

I am a gorgeous nerve ring with eyespots, a tongue,
      and a ribbon of teeth, rasping over rock

to scrap algae. Only the warring leviathan, though,
      could've imagined my beauty as a naval mine,

a weapon attached to a ship's hull before it blasts
      death. This limpet is *not* me.

I cannot bear the primitive thought—I am devoted
      to the splendor of this animal body of mine,

a lover with a three-chambered heart, bursting
      gametes into the brine to free-swim

then attach to a barnacled home, or to your seawall.
      You can see my homescar,

you've traced it before, your finger to stone, evidence
        I've wandered over this surface,

feeding with teeth stronger than steel, returning
        again, and again. Like you, I've worn a holy place

right here in your favorite spot. I've seen you
        sit and read a book, write a poem,

and stare at the ocean in your séance with a warming sea.
        Look away from your communion, poet.

At your feet, there's a raven's hat, or a stunning nipple,
        a limpet shell, striped and concave,

the old woman who gardened algae
        adorned in the bonnet-like shell, lives no more—

It is a gift now—wear it like you did as a child—
        a tiny hat on your thumb.

Drift Current

The poet is asking why
her footprints have filled up with the rising sea.

The poet wants to know
how shadows linger on the hillside all morning.

There she goes—the poet is looking
at the sandflea jumping on her shoe.

Why is it that the poet bothers the universe
with all her questions?

Does she really want to know
why the little neck clam burrows into mud?

Still Masked, Still Distant, Still

I searched for one spot in the universe
and I found it here, atop the seawall,
set back in the bay. This place of gratitude,

of gusts and rainfall, of leaves frolicking
in wind-breath, of the turning and churning
of seasons is what I offered to my body.

But how can I emerge from this dark seashore,
to join the others, not as the small animal
I have become, skittish when there's a harsh

voice or cough, not approachable yet.
I suppose I'll be the witness in the shadows
that I hide in, crouching low in the corners,

peering up behind the old mossy logs.
How can I show them, those who survived,
who are still hurting too,

there is a tenderness in me, that I want
to enter quietly, sit on the stones with them,
sing the old songs again.

My Father Departs With the Migrating Birds Heading North

It is a stretch to say it's spring,
   because just today, Winter
raised her hood, brushed frost from her shoulders.

But I am going to hold onto this afternoon light,
   this gift of the yellowish blur of sun
that lures my father with his binoculars

dressed in his bathrobe to sit out on the deck beside me.
   Here, we chew stories about kinfolk fishermen
and cheer on the kingfisher diving into the surface of sea.

We laugh at the fable of hummingbirds hitching rides
   north on the backs of sandhills.
What can I do to slow the wings of this day,

this flicker of sorrow arriving like the first hummingbird?
   I scatter the hour's seeds and toss them
into my belly of memory. This is it.

I am traveling through these days, bracing for the slough
   like a fragile riverbank in spring—
the icefloes are everywhere. I cannot stop

this momentum and when it does arrive
   it will be like thousands of migrating snow geese
lifting off the river flats in a white cloud of bird-thunder.

Dear Sitka Periwinkle,

I've always admired your four whorls, your spiral sculpturing, ridges and furrows, how your dark purple and gray bands catch light at low tide. I just wanted to say I know you're used to spawning several times per year, but things have changed. There are predators you must be aware of—that sea star—don't be fooled, friend. There's a red rock crab behind every boulder and the bullhead is not your friend. Still, go out and enjoy those foggy days, eat and drink your fill of diatoms, algae, lichen and rockweed. Have fun in the splash zone! Oh, Littorina sitkana, may the eelgrass always keep you safe.

NAVIFACE

The interface between atmosphere and ocean: sea surface.

The Skywatchers Wash Moondust From Your Face

Listen, the sandhills and your spirit
are following the last supermoon of the year,
honking in V-formation across the sky.

I feel the pull of this Harvest Moon,
how you are always in perigee, closer
to Earth than normal.

You are a constant—larger and brighter
than other fathers. Though a parade
of planets had lined up for this event,

on this planet, there are only two caretakers—
me, your daughter; and your son, my brother,
washing the sunken craters

of your lunar face as you wane.
In this rare year of four supermoons—
Full Buck Moon, Full Sturgeon,

the Blue Moon and the Harvest Moon,
at the end of salmon season,
when blueberries are windswept

from bushes, the fish smoked and jarred,
halibut in the freezer, jam and jelly
stacked on shelves, what better way

to mark the end of your orbit, alongside
your children, your magnificent shine
reflecting on their tear-bright faces.

From the Body That Is an Ocean

Some days I feel like I surround continents
        and churn a kaleidoscope of currents
on a mapmaker's chart.

I flip up krill and wash over kelp beds.
        Like me, you've begun in water.
But I remember everything,

the sharp-tuned heartbeat,
        voices gathering outside our tent wall.
I am not surprised by this knowing, still.

The slope of shore to tideline
        I walk every day is my escape. Moments
stolen from this unhinged world.

Here at the edge of the edge, everything is enormous.
        Some days the ocean is like silk,
somedays there are shadows beneath

the gray cloud's downcast gaze. These days,
        I remind myself it's enough
just to consider the water-strider,

in the stagnant stream beside my cabin
        who never considers puddle or ocean,
with her groves of leg hairs trapping air,

        walking atop her sea,
water-skipping toward the fallen dragonfly.

Inviting a poem into my house,

it sat with me while I rocked in my father's empty
recliner—as I rocked, little Brown Bird hopped

close to the open glass door, pecking at a bowl of seeds.
My father, a few weeks gone now, rocked in this same space

every day for a decade. This poem says that death will come
like hungry bear in autumn, and it did the end of September,

rustling in on the wind for our Grandpa Bear. The poem,
though, it speaks of death, is really about amazement,

and I consider my father as the poem's words bring him
clearly to my mind's light, standing him in the frame

of the open glass door with his binoculars pressed
to his face, discerning a storm spray—

if it's a williwaw or whale's breath. It isn't any wonder
that wonder kept him alive more years

than his damaged heart was due. If only to gaze
at more orange sunsets, at more sealions rising up

from the sea, ripping octopus, flinging their flesh
into the air. If only to write his first poem at age 76,

a poem about taking the time to just be. And me, here I am
rocking a pulse of moments,

reading words to an empty cabin, gathering up my curiosity,
enough to rise up to this daughterly duty from pondering

to help open a cardboard box, lift a black velvet bag
of my father's ashes into an anchor-etched urn.

Traces

My father's ghost, wearing his blue plaid
flannel shirt, sits beside me on the small metal
garden bench on my porch next to the ocean.

Sitting in the silence of morning, we are
watching for signs—ducks rafting
in the middle of the straits, the slick

ball-shaped head of the harbor seal,
a spout of vapor against the Etolin Island shore.
Everything is a sign of wonder. Somehow,

we exist in this space all together, my breath
can call a mosquito awake or my practice yoik
can beckon a whale nearer. And maybe this morning

even the sunlight on my face is whispering close.
But is it a memory that's gathering here or
something more? —I swear my father is patting

my knee, repeating his last words he ever said
to me—*thank you, daughter,* while the kingfisher
is diving headlong into the sea.

Imitations

You will no longer sit at twilight's edge
on your porch next to the sea and speak
        to crows heading to their roosts.

A flying crow once turned toward you
and your father, after your father
        squawked aloud at it,

and looked you both in the eye
and cawed out the same goodnight.
        You want to imitate your father,

mimicking the heron in the shade of
dusk now shadowing your porch.
        But your father's impact

on your life is a filament of vibrations
left undone, pulling loose the throat
        of the unknown you now face.

You wonder if you can allow your voice's
pulsing echo to mirror the sooty
        grouse's hooting, drum notes

against the rock bluffs in the bay
and send them back to you.
        Your father could.

This past summer, before he died,
you found him one day,
        sitting in a plastic chair

behind his cabin, surrounded by cedar,
hemlock, alder, and spruce.
        I'm listing to the birds he said,

his hearing aid adjusted; his head tilted.
He'd told you in all his years of unhearing,
       he'd missed bird sounds the most.

And already what you miss are his bluejay rasps
and thrush trills, the thumps and click
       of tongue and mouth-honks,

and his shrill fluttering past your cheek
as you both leaned over the porch rail,
       beneath you, a raft of ducks floating by—

father and daughter together, whistling
the string of the goldeneyes' flight.

A Drop in the Ocean

The spaces of my life between
waves, I carry like stones

in my pocket. Inside me, I am but
moon-formed shadows, a marine fog

slipping over the roof of an old house.
What has my life meant but a word

or two that's softened someone's mind,
or opened them up to see through

a frosted windshield, like a bear awakening
from a cave. Is it enough, every year

to venture out knee-deep in the ocean,
to plop oneself down and sit

on the popweed and sand, swirl the sea
around you with your hands,

knowing you belong to the unspoken,
something that even poets cannot name?

You're Invited to a Party for Loss

Ocean, as the earth rotates, you're invited
to the Earth's Bulge toward the moon.
I'm sure you'll want to attend because

you've been waiting for the invite, haven't you?
I can always tell when gravity is pulling at you.
Come party with us 6 adult children on the beach

at my fishcamp. Ocean, you know you want to
do your ancient dance in the direction of the moon,
so put on your seaweed party hat and stop by.

Your out-bulge is intoxicating and it's time
to get high. This party is happening at 9:00 am.
on June 30th. My father was always a morning person

and we humans are mourning too. Our step-mother's
and father's ashes we'll mix, bone and ash,
as an offering to you.

We'll be waiting for you under the waxing gibbous moon,
12 days young, under a charismatic sky brushed
with silver feather clouds.

We've booked the party music—the loons, the crows,
and the yellow-legs. We'll eat breakfast burritos, bacon
and cantaloupe, have coffee and hot cocoa and tea.

We'll entertain ourselves with stories and musings.
Ocean, our reverence will tamp the sand of laughter,
into a prayer and a poem of course.

And when you hold our loved ones, sweep them away,
it'll be more like a gentle rock and wave of your hand.
So how about it, Ocean, come rise and meet us

where the old log sits on the sand, where the eel grass
is swaying over the whale rock. We and the speckled limpet,
and the popweed and the worm wood will be waiting.

How to Pulse With the World Like It's the Last Day

Sometimes I keep time with the ocean.
But there's a rotating current of a warm algae bloom

and Moon is rolling over her mountain silhouettes again—
a song can sound like this. All movement. All breath.

Lately, the harbor seals keep watch, checking in
on me daily, pop up from the ocean's surface

to remind me of older times, how my ancestors
could chant with a twist and coil of squall.

This ocean rising, this earth unraveling

is my rhythm now. How can I exist as a part of this?
When in doubt—yoik. Sing up everything, they said.

When in doubt—visit the whale skull in your soggy winter garden.
When in doubt—pinch a handful of newly bloomed
        popweed from the beach.
When in doubt—get sandy, get wet, get muddy.
Leave the leaves in your hair. Don't brush off the sea.

My ancestors had a chant for everything—
Hum the sedge on the tundra. Catch the sharp edge

of a snowflake's melody on my tongue.
Sing up the ache growing in my winterhead, that sting

that makes me want to canoe to the edge of the world.
        Sing it from the throat of wind—
become the lichen swaying in the trees.

About the Author

Vivian Faith Prescott (She/Her) was born and raised in Wrangell, Kaachxana.áak'w, a small island in Southeastern Alaska in the Alexander Archipelago, also known as the Inside Passage. She writes and thrives at her family's fishcamp next to the sea on the land of the Shtax'heen Kwáan. She's a member of the Pacific Sámi Searvi and a founding member of the first LGBTQIA+ group on the island. She's the author of more than a dozen books, including poetry, fiction, and non-fiction. She's also a co-founder and co-facilitator of two Alaskan writers' groups: Blue Canoe Writers and the Drumlin Poets.

About the Cover Artist

Joanna Carlson Perea: Born and raised where the forest meets the sea in the remote fishing town of Cordova Alaska, Joanna has forever been mesmerized by the natural world. With a fondness for beachcombing for ocean treasures and exploring the intertidal zone to observe and appreciate the resilient marine life exposed when the tide recedes, Joanna draws much of her inspiration from the beauty and wonder of her coastal upbringing. Her vibrant and unique fiber art aims to capture and share how she perceives and honors Alaska's remarkable wildlife and scenery.

Sheila-Na-Gig Editions

www.ingramcontent.com/pod-product-compliance
Lightning Source LLC
Chambersburg PA
CBHW020742130626
46554CB00006B/2114